Copyright © 2015 Quote Octopus.com

Quote Octopus
Melbourne, Victoria, 3053
Australia
www.quoteoctopus.com

There is no life to be found in violence. Every act of violence brings us closer to death. Whether it's the mundane violence we do to our bodies by overeating toxic food or drink or the extreme violence of child abuse, domestic warfare, life-threatening poverty, addiction, or state terrorism.

bell hooks

Life is a series of baby steps along the way and if you add up these tiny little steps you take toward your goal, whatever it is, whether it's giving up something, a terrible addiction or trying to work your way through an illness. When you total up those baby steps you'd be amazed over the course of 10 years, the strides you've taken.

Hoda Kotb

Addiction isn't about substance - you aren't addicted to the substance, you are addicted to the alteration of mood that the substance brings.

Susan Cheever

All the suffering, stress, and addiction comes from not realizing you already are what you are looking for.

Jon Kabat-Zinn

If we want to address global warming, along with the other environmental problems associated with our continued rush to burn our precious fossil fuels as quickly as possible, we must learn to use our resources more wisely, kick our addiction, and quickly start turning to sources of energy that have fewer negative impacts.

David Suzuki

It is hard to understand addiction unless you have experienced it.

Ken Hensley

Every form of addiction is bad, no matter whether the narcotic be alcohol or morphine or idealism.

Carl Jung

Smoking sucks! The one thing I would say to my kid is, 'It's not just that it's bad for you. Do you want to spend the rest of your life fighting a stupid addiction to a stupid thing that doesn't even really give you a good buzz?'

Katherine Heigl

No one is immune from addiction; it afflicts people of all ages, races, classes, and professions.

Patrick J. Kennedy

The disaster in the Gulf was no accident. It was the result of years of oil money buying off politicians to lead to an unregulated and ill focused addiction to oil and drilling. The doomed fate of the local fisherman and the environment were foretold in the infamous chants of 'Drill, Baby, Drill.'

Robert Greenwald

Checking your ego, abandoning it, letting it go, is a huge part of recovery from addiction.

Susannah Grant

All sins tend to be addictive, and the terminal point of addiction is damnation.

W. H. Auden

I think I have an adrenaline addiction, no question about that.

Tom Waits

Negative freedom is freedom from - freedom from oppression, whether it's a colonial power or addiction to alcohol oppressing you. You need to be freed from negative freedom. Positive freedom is freedom for, freedom to be. And that's what's routinely ignored today.

Os Guinness

I started to write in about 1950; I was thirty-five at the time; there didn't seem to be any strong motivation. I simply was endeavoring to put down in a more or less straightforward journalistic style something about my experiences with addiction and addicts.

William S. Burroughs

We are taught to consume. And that's what we do. But if we realized that there really is no reason to consume, that it's just a mind set, that it's just an addiction, then we wouldn't be out there stepping on people's hands climbing the corporate ladder of success.

River Phoenix

Although the Chinese had used opium as a medicine, there was no widespread addiction before the British arrived.

Robert Trout

Making money is certainly the one addiction I cannot shake.

Felix Dennis

A lot of people think that addiction is a choice. A lot of people think it's a matter of will. That has not been my experience. I don't find it to have anything to do with strength.

Matthew Perry

It's an addiction. I love clothes. I like to go down Melrose and look in all the windows and I go to different flea markets. I have lots of costumes. You never know when you're going to have to dress up like a milkmaid from the 1600s.

Zooey Deschanel

Exercise is like an addiction. Once you're in it, you feel like your body needs it.

Elsa Pataky

Sometimes, when I hear people without experience of addiction blame addicts for their behaviour, I feel like saying to them: 'You simply don't understand - how can a child be held responsible for doing such a dreadful thing to himself?' But then again, at other times I have to acknowledge: it was done wilfully.

Will Self

It seems to me like Mother Nature's mercy and forgiveness have run dry, as we ceaselessly abuse her and take her for granted in order for us to continue our addiction to using fossil fuels. I've gotta say, I don't blame her. Not one bit.

Gloria Reuben

Practically every environmental problem we have can be traced to our addiction to fossil fuels, primarily oil.

Dennis Weaver

We may think there is willpower involved, but more likely... change is due to want power. Wanting the new addiction more than the old one. Wanting the new me in preference to the person I am now.

George A. Sheehan

Anything that you can become obsessed with, and you do so much that you don't do the things you need to do with family, friends, school, job - that can be an addiction. And texting absolutely can qualify.

Dale Archer

It's an addiction... and addiction is something I should know something about.

Keith Richards

I admire anyone who rids himself of an addiction.

Gene Tierney

This dark diction has become America's addiction.

Kanye West

A moderate addiction to money may not always be hurtful; but when taken in excess it is nearly always bad for the health.

Clarence Day

The model of ownership, in a society organized round mass consumption, is addiction.

Christopher Lasch

People who have never had an addiction don't understand how hard it can be.

Payne Stewart

My bulimia was my addiction. Hurting myself was my addiction... The music is what saved me. That's the only thing I can trust.

Nicole Scherzinger

Not everybody is comfortable with the idea that politics is a guilty addiction. But it is.

Hunter S. Thompson

In the summer of 1991, I was on the first Lollapalooza tour. Nightly, I would watch Jane's Addiction singer Perry Farrell go out in front of a sea of people and within minutes have all of them in the palm of his hand. I have never seen anything like it since.

Henry Rollins

She goes from one addiction to another. All are ways for her to not feel her feelings.

Ellen Burstyn

I am convinced now that virtually every destructive behavior and addiction I battled off and on for years was rooted in my (well-earned) insecurity.

Beth Moore

The effect of the mass media is not to elicit belief but to maintain the apparatus of addiction.

Christopher Lasch

Everybody smokes! Models, actresses, everyone! Don't they realize that it's gross? I understand it's an addiction, but it still pains me to see my friends do it.

Kirsten Dunst

Addiction is a really hard thing to kick.

Nikki Sixx

My addiction has always been beautiful women, being surrounded by them.

Corey Feldman

All behavioral or mood disorders - including depression, OCD, ADHD and addiction - have some neurochemical components, but sufferers can still work to overcome them.

Jeffrey Kluger

Secrecy, once accepted, becomes an addiction.

Edward Teller

When I have a creative insight, there is a high. I think back in the day, I made music as much as I did because it made me feel so good. I think you could argue that there is a creative addiction - but, you know, the healthy kind.

Lauryn Hill

Nothing is more singular about this generation than its addiction to music.

Allan Bloom

I think I have an addiction to pretty much everything. I mean, I have to be very careful with myself as far as that goes, which is why I have a support group around me consistently.

Corey Haim

Jane's Addiction has only put out new music when our hearts were in and when we had something to say creatively.

Dave Navarro

MySpace is an addiction.

Paulo Coelho

I remain convinced that obstinate addiction to ordinary language in our private thoughts is one of the main obstacles to progress in philosophy.

Bertrand Russell

I have made an art form of the interview. The French are the best interviewers, despite their addiction to the triad, like all Cartesians.

Orson Welles

People should watch out for three things: avoid a major addiction, don't get so deeply into debt that it controls your life, and don't start a family before you're ready to settle down.

James Taylor

It is time to end the discrimination against people who need treatment for chemical addiction. It is time for Congress to deal with our Nation's number one public health problem.

Jim Ramstad

I have the obsessiveness of someone who's a sober, recovering addict displacing his addiction. Except I never had the addiction.

John Mayer

Romantic love is an addiction.

Helen Fisher

I think golf is literally an addiction. I'm surprised there's not Golf Anonymous.

Larry David

The addiction to sports, therefore, in a peculiar degree marks an arrested development in man's moral nature.

Thorstein Veblen

I have a little bit of an addiction to work. So I'm always hiding in the bathroom with my Blackberry to work when I'm on holiday.

Penelope Cruz

Gang members have invariably grown up in broken, chaotic homes, often experiencing domestic violence; they have truanted from school and many have been formally excluded; and they live in neighbourhoods where worklessness, addiction and crime are rife.

Iain Duncan Smith

The end of my addiction to fame happened at the exact moment 'Roseanne' dropped out of the top ten, in the seventh of our nine seasons. It was mysteriously instantaneous!

Roseanne Barr

For a while, I had this uncontrollable urge - this addiction to danger. Now I look back and I think, 'Gee, what an idiot. I was risking my life just for the sensation of it.'

Steven Seagal

What I've learned to do is arrest my addiction - arrest it myself, so I don't get arrested.

Rodney King

I am trying to break free from my stripes addiction, but the pull is strong! I need help buying non-stripes.

Gillian Jacobs

There's a pattern when tours start - a pattern of infighting, of making up, of breaking up, of addiction. There's a pattern of going to jail. There's a pattern of passion for music.

Nikki Sixx

I was in my mid-40s. I was a bulimic, and I realized if I continue with this addiction of mine, I will not be able to continue doing my life. The older you get the more damage it does; it takes longer to recover from a binge. And it was very hard.

Jane Fonda

Trying to overcome addiction is one of the hardest things for a person to do. And the fact that I had to do it under the scrutiny of tabloid press at first made it seem even more difficult. But in fact, it oddly ended up being a plus. Because of the tabloid stuff, it wasn't like I could walk into a bar and order a drink.

Matthew Perry

I work with The National Center on Addiction and Substance Abuse at Columbia University. I sit proudly as one of only two recovering addicts on their board.

Jamie Lee Curtis

Contemplation is an alternative consciousness that refuses to identify with or feed what are only passing shows. It is the absolute opposite of addiction, consumerism or any egoic consciousness.

Richard Rohr

I know being pregnant and giving birth is the most wonderful thing on Earth. I know that after you have a baby, there is a sense of addiction, a need to have another. It's biological.

Janine di Giovanni

I have an addiction to caffeine.

Bill Ayers

I really love to act; I love everything about it. I've never had this addiction to being known. I mean, sure, if you go into acting, there's part of you that is saying, 'I want attention' but I was brought up to work to deserve attention, and it is the work, not the trappings that are important.

Christopher Meloni

The Gillard government must give up its addiction to wasteful spending borrowing and taxing.

Julie Bishop

No addiction is good.

Jose Mujica

Ottolenghi sells lots of delicious sweet things, but my daily addiction is their unbelievable dark chocolate salted caramel biscuits. They're the best things in the world - I go through half a packet every night. I bring them out after pudding at dinner parties.

Trinny Woodall

We have seen what the dependence and addiction to foreign oil has done to us economically.

Ron Kind

My father left when I was really young, but he's still living. There are things I wish I'd said that I didn't and I don't think I'll ever get the opportunity to say. He's battled addiction problems his entire life. I wish things were different. I wish there were a way my son could know him, know the good parts of him.

Sarah Shahi

My mum thought my TV and film addiction was laziness. If you're an immigrant, you know you'll never be an accepted part of society, but you hope your children will be, and you try to make them essential to the community in a practical way - being a doctor or a lawyer. Acting was beyond their comprehension.

Sanjeev Bhaskar

The need to help spread democracy and the ability to do that will be much greater if we break this addiction to oil, which gives the oil princes and sultans the power in the Mideast.

Jay Inslee

I wanted to do an episode about Chuck having a gambling problem. I wanted to portray my addiction on the show. But I think it's a little edgy for Saturday night.

Fisher Stevens

I had always turned it down-to me, smoking pot was absolutely the worst thing in the world. I thought of it as an addiction, and all my friends who smoked it, I felt they really needed help.

Tommy Rettig

When the President was asked about global warming at a public appearance yesterday, he responded by talking about America's addiction to oil. You make the connection.

Gwen Ifill

Years of research in psychology has shown that rewards and punishments can be very effective in changing behavior. But, at the same time, they can create an addiction to rewards and punishments.

Barry Schwartz

I'm always very stressed about making a new proposition every season. But in a way, it's a kind of addiction.

Nicolas Ghesquiere

I have a bit of a traveling addiction, and, ah, yeah. I went to, ah, Bali this summer.

Fisher Stevens

Twitter is a real addiction, like the color of it, the process of it.

Earl Sweatshirt

With the implementation of the Affordable Care Act and the Mental Health Parity and Addiction Equity Act, more people will have insurance coverage and, in principle, be eligible for more care.

Thomas R. Insel

I was happier when pursuing success than I was when savoring its fruits; the attraction, perhaps the addiction, was in the process, as much as in its end.

Michael Steinhardt

I started riding bikes when I was really young, but I stopped when I was 19 because my mother asked me to, so I stopped riding for 35 years and now I'm just addicted. It is my only addiction.

Mark Boone Junior

Money doesn't mind if we say it's evil, it goes from strength to strength. It's a fiction, an addiction, and a tacit conspiracy.

Martin Amis

We humans have become dependent on plastic for a range of uses, from packaging to products. Reducing our use of plastic bags is an easy place to start getting our addiction under control.

David Suzuki

I always think I am one of the millions and millions of people that struggles with an addiction to food. I don't know how to relax, that's my problem.

Carnie Wilson

I love making people laugh. It's an addiction and it's probably dysfunctional, but I am addicted to it and there's no greater pleasure for me than sitting in a theater and feeling a lot of people losing control of themselves.

Jay Roach

I had an addiction to play baseball.

Pete Rose

I think we need to educate our doctors about addiction.

Matthew Perry

We must move in our recovery from one addiction to another for two major reasons: first, we have not recognized and treated the underlying addictive process, and second, we have not accurately isolated and focused upon the specific addictions.

Anne Wilson Schaef

I have a severe addiction to 'Angry Birds.' I always tell myself, 'One more game...' But then there's always another and another and another.

Kevin Nealon

Over-eating is the addiction choice of carers, and that's why it's come to be regarded as the lowest-ranking of all the addictions.

Caitlin Moran

I'm a former bulimic myself and it's a horrible, horrible addiction.

Janice Dickinson

Let us build a 21st-century rural economy of cutting-edge companies and technologies that lead us to energy and food security. Such an investment will revitalize rural America, re-establish our moral leadership on climate security and eliminate our addiction to foreign oil.

Tom Vilsack

Stand-up, for me, is really more of an addiction, so you have to feed the beast whenever you can.

John Oliver

If I have one addiction in life, it's probably food.

Liam Hemsworth

Addiction is a terrible thing.

Jamie Dornan

At school, I was only allowed four sweets every Wednesday, so I've developed an addiction.

Trinny Woodall

I don't have, you know, an 'overcoming addiction' story, other than the guitar itself, and I haven't overcome that. I don't have a jail time, you know, story, or any arrests.

Brad Paisley

Meeting Perry Farrel was kind of cool. He's such an icon, and I was such a fan of Jane's Addiction.

James Mercer

'Higher Power' was the result of a personal experience: a friend of mine who went through the process of addiction and recovery. It's a very, very tough thing - very easy to become addicted and very, very hard to become a recovering addict.

Tom Scholz

I have to be careful with surfing. It's still an addiction to me. It's all I want to do, and that's the big dilemma I have with it.

Chris Carter

Marijuana is a much bigger part of the American addiction problem than most people - teens or adults - realize.

John Walters

Pomegranate juice has staying power. It's not a fad. Once people have tasted POM Wonderful, they say they are addicted - and it's a good addiction to have.

Lynda Resnick

I've triumphed over addiction.

Tatum O'Neal

I've become very interested in the spectrum of political discourse as seen on the cable news channels that are conveniently right in a row on my cable provider's dial. I can flip from Fox to CNN to HLN to MSNBC, and I find myself at night flipping it back and forth through them, and it's something of an addiction.

Chris Carter

Sugar is more present in America or England than it is in France. I think there is an addiction to sweetness.

Pierre Dukan

That is the one single word that the food industry hates: 'addiction.' They much prefer words like 'crave-ability' and 'allure.'

Michael Moss

Collection is an addiction.

Judith Miller

In a storm of struggles, I have tried to control the elements, clasp the fist tight so as to protect self and happiness. But stress can be an addiction, and worry can be our lunge for control, and we forget the answer to this moment is always yes because of Christ.

Ann Voskamp

At the end of a project I get very weird, you know, in my head because I'm not doing it. It's like an addiction. I have to do it.

Roberta Williams

You can change a person's life in an instant; put him in a movie, and you start thinking differently, you want to be in another movie. It's like an addiction almost.

Dennis Farina

Despite the previous efforts of Congresses, our addiction to foreign oil, as the President stated, is greater today than ever before. That dependency is a threat to our national security, and we must address that threat.

Jim Costa

Dyeing my hair has become a kind of addiction. I can't see myself as anything other than blond. Once you go blond, you stay blond forever.

Valeria Mazza

I know in my soul when something feels like a sell out and I think for me, I knew that if I did the Jane's Addiction reunion thing, that I would feel like a sell out. That's how it would feel to me.

Eric Avery

We clearly need to break our addiction on Saudi Arabian oil that is a security threat to the United States.

Jay Inslee

Americans' addiction to sports, with the NFL at the top, is based on the excitement generated by the potential for the unexpected great play which can only happen with honest competition from great athletes.

Arlen Specter

Life without oil, in fact, would be so different that it is frightening to contemplate. We are addicted, and it is no comfortable addiction.

James Buchan

I have a slight addiction to Diet Coke, and, of course, I absolutely shouldn't touch it because it makes the kidneys work really hard.

Sue Townsend

It wasn't a deliberate decision to become a poet. It was something I found myself doing - and loving. Language became an addiction.

Yusef Komunyakaa

For decades the American people have had an addiction to oil and gas.

Lee H. Hamilton

I started producing work with an ecstatic addiction.

Ben Nicholson

I am glad that Wimbledon is my last slam. I love the atmosphere and courts of SW19, and it is an addiction, which I will find tough to give up.

Mahesh Bhupathi

I taught myself computer. Then Macintosh came along, and it became a really bad addiction. If I wasn't in show business, I'd have pocket protectors growing out of my chest. I do everything on it. It's kinda sick.

Jeff Dunham

Method involves a slavish addiction to laws, and we can only aspire to anarchy.

Robert Pinsky

When I was at school, I wanted to join the army. At college, I started acting in college plays, and it became a kind of addiction. I was very shy when I was at school, but the plays seemed to give voice to my feelings.

Om Puri

Comics are in my blood. It's my strange addiction, and I love it.

Roberto Aguirre-Sacasa

I used to dress like Roger Taylor when I was ten because I thought he was cool. In high school, I used to dress like Stephen Perkins from Jane's Addiction because I thought he was cool. You just want to be those guys when you're that age.

Taylor Hawkins

I learned how to play guitar by playing along to Jane's Addiction records and Smashing Pumpkins records, things you can totally hear if you listen to my guitar.

Chino Moreno

That's it. With equal parts regret and relief, the Jane's Addiction experiment is at an end.

Eric Avery

We need to reduce or at least limit U.S. demand for oil as quickly as possible, and we need to develop new technologies that can further help address our addiction to oil in the future.

Sherwood Boehlert

www.ingramcontent.com/pod-product-compliance
Lightning Source LLC
Chambersburg PA
CBHW061948280526
45787CB00004B/1773